This book is dedicated to all the clients that I have worked with over the years. I have been fortunate enough to work with a diverse group of clients with many different needs. I feel like I have given every client some effective tools, but I have also learned something from every single client.

TABLE OF CONTENTS

Introduction

Congratulations on the first steps towards living in mindfulness.

Understanding how stress impacts the brain and body allows us to learn how

to reduce the impact in a way that brings a calm state of being. Many people

know how stress impacts their daily life; they simply don't know how to

manage the stress in a healthy way. This journey towards living mindfully

provides useful strategies to reduce stress.

This book provides useful information, including how stress activates

the sympathetic nervous system, flooding the body with adrenaline and

cortisol (the stress hormones). It also provides effective tools to

counterbalance those hormones by activating the parasympathetic nervous

system to release dopamine and serotonin (the feel-good hormones).

While we may not always have control over the stressors in our daily

lives, we can control how we respond to them. Choosing healthy ways to

respond, rather than react, to situations allows us to reduce the impact of stress on our brain, body, and behaviors. Reacting emotionally to stressful events becomes a negative behavior pattern over time, which results in increased likelihood of experiencing anxiety and/or depression. Learning how to respond to these stressors in a healthy way results in a positive behavior pattern over time. This results in becoming better equipped to maintain a more peaceful state of being.

I have worked in the mental health field for 20 years, and I have worked with so many different people ages 8-65. I have learned how stress impacts the brain, body, and behaviors through work experience, earning 2 master's degrees and a PhD, and participating in trainings and certifications to increase my understanding of how the nervous system responds to stress. Mindfulness isn't just something we do; it's a way of life.

PART I: Understanding How Stress Impacts the Brain, Body, and Behaviors

In order to learn how to manage stress in our lives, we should first understand how stress can impact our brain, body, and behaviors. We can become stuck in a negative cycle of behavior as our stress response, especially when we do not have adequate, effective strategies to manage the stress response in a health way.

Chapter One: The Impact of Stress

In this chapter, we delve into the profound effects of stress on both the brain and body. From elevated cortisol levels to the activation of the sympathetic nervous system, we explore the intricate ways stress can compromise our well-being.

Stress triggers the release of stress hormones, like adrenaline and cortisol, which activates the sympathetic nervous system. This response prepares the body for a "fight or flight" reaction, increasing heart rate, dilating pupils, and redirecting blood flow to vital organs. Long-term exposure to stress hormones, such as cortisol, can have adverse effects on both the brain and overall health. Chronic stress may lead to:

Impaired Cognitive Function

Prolonged cortisol exposure can impair memory, concentration, and decision-making. It can impact relationships, work, and school if we don't have strategies to counteract the stress hormones and their effect on us.

Mental Health Issues

Stress can increase the risk of developing anxiety, depression, and other mental health disorders due to alterations in neurotransmitter levels. If we learn effective stress management tools, we can decrease the risk of developing mental health issues.

Sleep Disturbances

Disrupted sleep patterns and insomnia may result from elevated stress hormones. You may have difficulty falling asleep or staying asleep. You may sleep too much or not enough. Even if you get the sleep hours in, you may wake up feeling fatigued.

Weakened Immune System

Chronic stress can suppress the immune system, making individuals more susceptible to illnesses.

Cardiovascular Issues

Elevated stress hormones contribute to high blood pressure and increased risk of heart disease.

Digestive Problems

Stress can lead to gastrointestinal issues, causing or exacerbating conditions like irritable bowel syndrome (IBS). Stress can result in eating too much or not enough.

Weight Gain or Weight Loss

Stress hormones can influence appetite, potentially leading to overeating and weight gain, especially around the abdominal area. It can also lead to decreased appetite and weight loss.

Accelerated Aging

Long-term stress may contribute to premature aging by affecting cellular processes. Managing stress through techniques like mindfulness, exercise, nutrition, and adequate sleep is crucial for mitigating these negative health impacts. Stress, that ever-present companion in the human experience, weaves a complex tapestry of effects on both the brain and body. As we navigate the challenges of daily life, stressors trigger a cascade of physiological and neurological responses that reverberate throughout our entire being.

Stress and the Brain:

The brain, our intricate command center, bears the brunt of stress's impact. The amygdala, a key player in our emotional responses, becomes hyperactive, scanning for threats and sounding the alarm. Meanwhile, the prefrontal cortex, responsible for rational decision-making, grapples with reduced functionality under the weight of stress hormones.

Chronic stress takes a toll on the hippocampus, a region vital for memory and learning. Prolonged exposure to stress hormones impairs neurogenesis—the birth of new neurons—diminishing the brain's resilience and cognitive flexibility.

The Hormonal Symphony:

Stress orchestrates a hormonal symphony, with cortisol playing a leading role. Released in response to stress, cortisol mobilizes energy reserves and sharpens the senses. However, chronic elevation of cortisol levels becomes a double-edged sword. It disrupts sleep patterns, weakens the immune system, and contributes to the accumulation of visceral fat.

The intricate interplay of stress hormones also affects the endocrine system. Imbalances in hormones like adrenaline and noradrenaline can lead to heightened blood pressure, potentially paving the way for cardiovascular issues.

The Cellular Consequences:

At the cellular level, stress can accelerate the aging process. Telomeres, the protective caps at the ends of chromosomes, tend to shorten more rapidly under chronic stress. This cellular aging is associated with a higher risk of various health problems, from cardiovascular diseases to neurodegenerative conditions.

Unraveling the Mind-Body Connection:

The mind-body connection, once dismissed as mere metaphor, is increasingly substantiated by scientific findings. Stress serves as a bridge between psychological well-being and physical health. Mental distress can manifest in physical symptoms, from tension headaches to gastrointestinal discomfort.

Conversely, physical well-being can influence mental health. Engaging in regular exercise, for instance, not only strengthens the body but also acts as a buffer against the detrimental effects of stress on the mind.

Coping Strategies and Resilience:

Acknowledging the profound effects of stress prompts a quest for effective coping strategies. Mindfulness practices, such as meditation and yoga, offer tools for reining in the runaway thoughts that accompany stress. Social support, too, emerges as a powerful antidote, fostering resilience in the face of life's challenges.

In the labyrinth of stress, understanding its impact on the brain and body becomes a compass for navigating towards well-being. Through this awareness, we empower ourselves to cultivate resilience, embracing a balance that fortifies both our mental and physical realms.

Chapter Summary/Key Takeaways

- Stress results in the release of adrenaline and cortisol, the stress hormones

- Under stress, we can experience change in appetite, sleep disturbances, and changes in our energy levels.

- Chronic stress can result in health problems, such as digestive issues, heart problems, and impaired cognition.

In the next chapter, we will explore how the brain responds to stress.

Chapter Two: Unraveling the Brain's Response

Understanding the neurological aspects of stress, we explore how chronic stress can reshape the brain, affecting memory, concentration, and emotional regulation. Discover the science behind the amygdala's role in the stress response and its impact on decision-making.

Stress, that ubiquitous force weaving through the fabric of human experience, has a profound impact on our neurological landscape. Delving into the intricate workings of the brain provides a lens through which we can better comprehend the physiological responses to stress and its far-reaching effects.

The Brain's Command Center

At the epicenter of stress response is the amygdala, a small almond-shaped structure nestled deep within the brain. Acting as the brain's sentinel, the amygdala is primed to detect potential threats, triggering the release of stress hormones when it perceives danger.

The HPA Axis Dance

The hypothalamus-pituitary-adrenal (HPA) axis orchestrates the body's stress symphony. A cascade of signals initiates in the hypothalamus, signaling the pituitary gland to release adrenocorticotropic hormone (ACTH). This hormonal relay prompts the adrenal glands to unleash cortisol, the body's primary stress hormone. Elevated cortisol levels prepare the body for the "fight or flight" response, mobilizing energy reserves and sharpening focus.

Cortical Conundrums

The prefrontal cortex, the brain's command center for decision-making and emotional regulation, also plays a pivotal role in stress modulation. Chronic stress can impair prefrontal cortex function, hampering our ability to think clearly and make rational decisions. This cognitive fog contributes to a heightened state of perceived threat, perpetuating the stress cycle.

Neurotransmitter Tango

Neurotransmitters, the brain's chemical messengers, further entwine stress in the neural tapestry. The delicate balance between excitatory neurotransmitters like glutamate and inhibitory ones like gamma-aminobutyric acid (GABA) determines the overall neural tone. Chronic stress disrupts this equilibrium, fostering conditions conducive to anxiety and mood disorders.

Neuroplasticity's Dilemma

The brain's remarkable ability to adapt, known as neuroplasticity, can be a double-edged sword in the context of stress. While the brain can rewire itself in response to stressors, maladaptive changes may occur, contributing to conditions like post-traumatic stress disorder (PTSD). Understanding the interplay between stress and neuroplasticity is crucial in developing targeted interventions.

The Chronic Stress Saga

Prolonged exposure to stress can induce structural changes in the hippocampus, a region vital for memory and emotional regulation. Shrinkage of the hippocampus has been observed in individuals grappling with chronic stress, offering insights into the neural underpinnings of stress-related disorders.

Beyond the Brain: The Body's Stress Symphony

While the brain takes center stage in the stress narrative, it's essential to recognize stress as a holistic experience involving the entire body. The intricate interplay between the central nervous system and peripheral systems, such as the immune and cardiovascular systems, underscores stress's systemic impact.

In unraveling the neurological aspects of stress, we gain not only a deeper comprehension of the brain's response but also insights into potential avenues for intervention. The journey through the neural landscape of stress is ongoing, with each discovery shedding light on the intricate connections between mind and body in the face of life's challenges.

Chapter Summary/Key Takeaways

- Stress can shrink the brain in 2 areas; the hippocampus and the prefrontal cortex.

- Stress can impact concentration, memory, and the ability to regulate emotions.

- Stress impacts the entire body, not just the brain.

In the next chapter, we will explore how stress impacts the body.

Chapter Three: The Body's Symphony of Stress

This chapter unravels the physiological consequences of stress, from tense muscles and shallow breathing to compromised immune function. We shed light on the intricate dance between hormones and organs, illustrating the toll chronic stress takes on our overall health.

Stress, both acute and chronic, exerts a profound impact on the human body, triggering a cascade of physiological responses that can have lasting consequences. This chapter delves into the intricate ways in which stress affects various systems, exploring the interplay between the brain, endocrine system, and immune response.

The Stress Response: A Survival Mechanism

When confronted with a stressor, the body activates the "fight, flight, freeze, or fawn" response, orchestrated by the sympathetic nervous system. This results in the release of stress hormones, such as cortisol and adrenaline, preparing the body for imminent challenges. While this response is crucial for survival, prolonged activation can lead to detrimental effects on health.

Brain-Body Communication

The brain plays a central role in the stress response, with the hypothalamus-pituitary-adrenal (HPA) axis serving as a key mediator. Chronic stress can dysregulate this axis, contributing to elevated cortisol levels that, over time, impact cognitive function, memory, and emotional well-being.

Cardiovascular Consequences

The cardiovascular system bears a significant burden during periods of stress. Increased heart rate, elevated blood pressure, and altered blood flow are common responses. Prolonged stress may contribute to atherosclerosis and an increased risk of cardiovascular diseases.

Endocrine Disruption

Stress disrupts the delicate balance of hormones in the endocrine system, affecting reproductive health, metabolism, and growth. Dysregulation of sex hormones can lead to fertility issues, irregular menstrual cycles, and even contribute to conditions like polycystic ovary syndrome (PCOS).

Immune System Suppression

Stress has a suppressive effect on the immune system, compromising the body's ability to defend against pathogens. This immunosuppression increases susceptibility to infections and may contribute to the exacerbation of chronic inflammatory conditions.

Gastrointestinal Impact

The gut-brain axis highlights the bidirectional communication between the brain and the gastrointestinal system. Stress can lead to disturbances in gut function, exacerbating conditions like irritable bowel syndrome (IBS) and inflammatory bowel disease (IBD).

Coping Mechanisms and Health Interventions

Understanding the physiological consequences of stress underscores the importance of effective coping mechanisms. Lifestyle interventions, such as regular exercise, mindfulness practices, and social support, play a crucial role in mitigating the negative effects of stress on the body.

In conclusion, stress is a pervasive aspect of modern life, and its physiological consequences extend beyond momentary discomfort. A comprehensive approach to stress management, encompassing both psychological and physiological strategies, is essential for maintaining overall health and well-being.

Chapter Summary/Key Takeaways

- The stress response is a survival mechanism.

- Stress can impact our biological systems involving the brain, endocrine, and immune systems.

- Stress is a natural part of life but can have lasting psychological and physiological problems if we don't learn to manage stress effectively.

In the next chapter, we will discuss how to manage stress to maintain a calm state of being.

PART II: Managing the Stress

Managing stress is a much easier task when we understand how stress impacts the brain, body, and behaviors. Mindfulness is a great way to manage stress, however everyone is different. This means that there are many effective strategies, but not everyone responds to techniques in the same way. It is important to experiment to find the strategies that work best for you. For instance, activating the senses is a grounding strategy that works well. Some people like a specific type of music to activate hearing, while others like a different type of music. The strategy is the same, but the music is different. The important part is knowing that you may need to experiment.

Chapter Four: Mindfulness Steppingstones

Introducing the concept of mindfulness, we explore how it serves as steppingstones towards cultivating a calmer state of being. Mindfulness practices, such as meditation and mindful breathing, become essential tools for engaging the parasympathetic nervous system.

In the journey toward cultivating a calmer state of being, mindfulness emerges as a powerful and transformative tool. As we navigate the complexities of modern life, the practice of mindfulness serves as a series of steppingstones, guiding us towards a serene and centered existence.

Awareness of the Present Moment

Mindfulness invites us to anchor ourselves in the present moment, releasing the burdens of the past and the anxieties of the future. By becoming acutely aware of our thoughts, emotions, and sensations in the here and now, we lay the foundation for a calmer mental landscape.

Embracing Non-Judgmental Observation

In the practice of mindfulness, we learn to observe our thoughts without judgment. Rather than labeling them as good or bad, we cultivate a neutral awareness. This non-judgmental stance liberates us from the cycle of self-criticism and fosters a sense of acceptance, a key element in achieving a tranquil state of mind.

Cultivating Mindful Breathing

The breath serves as an ever-present anchor in the realm of mindfulness. By paying deliberate attention to our breath, we connect with the rhythm of life. Deep, intentional breathing becomes a source of inner calm, allowing us to navigate challenges with a composed demeanor.

Developing Emotional Regulation

Mindfulness empowers us to witness our emotions as passing phenomena, providing a space for reflection before reaction. Through consistent practice, we develop the capacity to regulate our emotional responses, fostering resilience in the face of life's inevitable storms.

Quieting the Mental Chatter

The mind is a constant generator of thoughts, many of which contribute to stress and restlessness. Mindfulness teaches us to observe this mental chatter without becoming entangled in it. Gradually, the mind finds stillness, paving the way for a quieter and more serene inner landscape.

Connecting with the Senses

Engaging the senses mindfully enhances our connection with the present moment. Whether savoring the taste of food, feeling the warmth of sunlight, or appreciating the beauty of nature, such sensory awareness grounds us in the richness of our immediate experience, fostering a deep sense of calm. Music is a great way to ground yourself. Some people like to activate the sense of smell with scented candles or scented plug-ins; some like scented body lotion or spray. With sense of touch, some people hold an ice cube in their hand and let it melt; some like to put a piece of ice in their mouth.

Mindful Action and Intention

As mindfulness permeates our daily activities, we bring a conscious awareness to each action. Whether walking, eating, or working, we infuse intention into our activities. This mindful engagement fosters a sense of purpose and fulfillment, contributing to an overall state of tranquility.

In essence, mindfulness serves as a series of steppingstones, guiding us toward a calmer state of being. Through these practices, we transform our relationship with the present moment, our emotions, and the world around us. The journey is ongoing, but with each mindful step, we inch closer to the serene and centered existence we seek.

Chapter Summary/Key Takeaways

- Mindfulness isn't a cookie-cutter approach. The strategy may be the same, but the actual method/type may differ.

- Some people use one or two strategies; some people use a combination of several strategies throughout the day. Finding the strategies that work best for you is key.

- Mindfulness is an ongoing journey that teaches us how to regulate our emotions so that we are equipped to manage stress.

In the next chapter, you will learn about the parasympathetic nervous system.

Chapter Five: The Parasympathetic Nervous System Unveiled

Delving into the intricacies of the parasympathetic nervous system, we uncover its role as the body's natural relaxation response. Learn how mindfulness practices act as catalysts, promoting rest and recovery, and counterbalancing the detrimental effects of chronic stress.

In the intricate orchestra of the human body, the parasympathetic nervous system emerges as the conductor of tranquility, orchestrating a harmonious melody of relaxation and restoration. This chapter delves into the pivotal role played by the parasympathetic nervous system, often hailed as the body's natural relaxation response.

The Autonomic Harmony

The autonomic nervous system, a dynamic duo comprising the sympathetic and parasympathetic branches, choreographs the involuntary functions that keep us alive. While the sympathetic system takes the stage during times of stress, arousal, and action, the parasympathetic system gracefully steps in to restore equilibrium.

Unveiling the PNS: A Symphony of Rest

Picture the parasympathetic nervous system as a skilled maestro guiding the body towards serenity. Activated during moments of calm and repose, the PNS oversees a cascade of physiological changes, inducing a state often referred to as "rest and digest." Heart rate decelerates, breathing becomes slow and deep, and digestion takes center stage.

The Vagus Nerve: Pioneering Calm

At the heart of the parasympathetic symphony lies the vagus nerve, a wandering nerve that traverses the body, connecting various organs to the brain. Often dubbed the "wandering nerve," the vagus nerve is a key player in transmitting the calming signals that prompt the body to unwind.

Mind-Body Connection: Bridging Thoughts and Physiology

The parasympathetic system acts as a mediator in the intricate dance between mind and body. Stressful thoughts can trigger the sympathetic system, while calm and positive thoughts activate the parasympathetic system, showcasing the profound link between mental well-being and physiological responses.

The Healing Touch: Immune Boost and Cellular Repair

As the parasympathetic system takes charge, it not only fosters a sense of relaxation but also promotes healing at a cellular level. Enhanced immune function, improved digestion, and cellular repair are some of the transformative effects attributed to the PNS, emphasizing its role in maintaining overall health.

Cultivating the Relaxation Response

Understanding the parasympathetic nervous system invites us to explore practices that nurture its influence. Mindfulness, deep breathing, and activities promoting a sense of safety and connection foster an environment conducive to the activation of the PNS, facilitating the body's innate ability to relax and rejuvenate.

In conclusion, the parasympathetic nervous system stands as the unsung hero of relaxation, orchestrating a symphony of physiological responses that not only alleviate stress but also promote holistic well-being. Unlocking the potential of this natural relaxation response opens doors to a world where balance and tranquility prevail, allowing us to navigate the complexities of life with grace and resilience.

Chapter Summary/Key Takeaways

- The parasympathetic nervous system facilitates the release of dopamine and serotonin.

- The parasympathetic nervous system restores equilibrium.

- Mindfulness strategies activate the parasympathetic nervous system and return us to a calm state.

In the next chapter, there will be an exploration of ways to build mindful habits in our daily lives.

Chapter Six: **Building Mindful Habits**

This chapter provides practical tips for incorporating mindfulness into daily life. From brief mindful pauses to more extended meditation sessions, readers discover how to establish habits that support mental and physical well-being.

In the hustle and bustle of modern life, integrating mindfulness into our daily routines can be a transformative practice. Mindfulness, at its core, involves paying attention to the present moment without judgment. In this chapter, we'll explore practical ways to infuse mindfulness into various aspects of your daily life.

Morning Rituals

Begin your day with intentionality. Instead of rushing through your morning routine, savor each moment. Notice the sensation of water during your shower, the aroma of your breakfast, and the warmth of sunlight. As you engage in these activities, focus on your breath, anchoring yourself in the present.

Mindful Commuting

Whether you're driving, walking, or using public transportation, commuting offers an opportunity for mindfulness. Shift your attention from stressors to the sights, sounds, and sensations around you. Notice the colors of the sky, the rhythm of your footsteps, or the hum of the engine. This simple shift can turn a daily chore into a mindful journey.

Mindful Eating

In a fast-paced world, meals are often hurried affairs. Instead, turn eating into a mindful practice. Engage your senses—savor the flavors, appreciate the textures, and be fully present with each bite. Put away distractions, like screens, and focus on the nourishment your food provides.

Workplace Mindfulness

Work can be a breeding ground for stress. Introduce brief mindfulness pauses into your workday. Take a few minutes to focus on your breath, allowing yourself to reset. When faced with a challenging task, approach it with a clear and calm mind.

Mindfulness at work not only enhances productivity but also fosters a positive work environment.

Mindful Technology Use

Technology often consumes our attention. Set boundaries for screen time, and periodically disconnect to reconnect with the world around you. When using technology, do so with purpose—whether it's sending an email or scrolling through social media, be aware of your intention and attention.

Mindful Reflection

End your day with a moment of reflection. Review the events of the day without judgment. What moments brought joy, and what challenges did you face? Acknowledge them without attachment. Consider keeping a gratitude journal to capture positive moments and cultivate gratitude.

Mindful Sleep

As you prepare for sleep, transition from the day's activities to a state of rest. Practice relaxation techniques, such as deep breathing or gentle stretching. Allow your mind to settle, releasing any lingering thoughts. Approach sleep as a mindful transition, promoting restful and rejuvenating nights.

Incorporating mindfulness into your daily life is a gradual process. Be patient with yourself and remember that each moment offers a new opportunity to be present. As you weave mindfulness into your routines, you'll likely find a greater sense of peace, clarity, and fulfillment in the tapestry of your daily life.

Chapter Summary/Key Takeaways

- Mindfulness involves being present in the current moment and enjoying it.

- Mindfulness can be used in many different areas of life, including our commute to and from work, eating, and in the workplace.

- Mindful reflection is important at the end of the day; it can assist us in transitioning to bedtime with a positive frame of mind.

In the next chapter, we relate Mindfulness to real-life situations.

Chapter Seven: Mindfulness in Action

Real-life stories illustrate the transformative power of mindfulness. Readers witness individuals navigating stress, applying mindfulness steppingstones to redirect their neural pathways, and fostering resilience in the face of life's challenges.

In the realm of everyday lives, the transformative power of mindfulness reveals itself through profound stories of individuals who embarked on a journey of self-discovery and resilience. These real-life narratives serve as testaments to the profound impact mindfulness can have on one's well-being.

Sarah's Serenity

Sarah, a corporate executive overwhelmed by the demands of her high-stakes job, found solace in mindfulness meditation. Through consistent practice, she learned to navigate stress with grace, fostering a calm demeanor even in the face of chaos. This newfound serenity not only improved her mental health but also positively influenced her professional relationships, leading to a more collaborative and productive work environment.

James' Journey Through Grief

James, grappling with the loss of a loved one, turned to mindfulness as a means of coping with grief. Through mindfulness practices, he learned to acknowledge and accept his emotions without being overwhelmed. This allowed him to gradually heal, finding peace amid the storm of sorrow. James' story illustrates how mindfulness can provide a guiding light through the darkest times.

Maria's Mindful Parenting

Struggling with the demands of parenthood, Maria embraced mindfulness to cultivate patience and presence. By incorporating mindfulness into her daily interactions with her children, she forged deeper connections and nurtured a harmonious family dynamic. Maria's journey exemplifies the transformative impact mindfulness can have on relationships and the cultivation of a nurturing family environment.

Tom's Triumph Over Anxiety

Tom, plagued by chronic anxiety, discovered the power of mindfulness to break free from the cycle of worry. Through mindfulness-based stress reduction techniques, he gained the tools to observe his thoughts without being consumed by them.

Tom's story serves as a beacon of hope for those navigating the

tumultuous waters of anxiety, illustrating that mindfulness can be

a lifeline to tranquility.

Emma's Emotional Resilience

Emma, facing setbacks in her personal and professional

life, turned to mindfulness to build emotional resilience. By

embracing the present moment and reframing challenges as

opportunities for growth, she transformed adversity into a

catalyst for positive change. Emma's narrative underscores how

mindfulness can empower individuals to navigate life's

complexities with grace and resilience.

In each of these stories, the transformative power of

mindfulness is palpable, demonstrating its capacity to instigate positive change in diverse aspects of life. As these individuals discovered, the journey inward through mindfulness not only fosters personal well-being but also ripples outward, influencing relationships, work dynamics, and the overall quality of life. These stories stand as reminders that amidst life's challenges, the practice of mindfulness can be a guiding force, leading to profound and enduring transformation.

Chapter Summary/Key Takeaways

- Mindfulness can be an important part of our daily life as illustrated in this chapter.

- Mindfulness can be used in many difficult areas of life, including managing anxiety, grief, and a multitude of other situations.

- Mindfulness can be powerful and transformative when we incorporate it into our life.

In the next chapter, we relate Mindfulness to real-life situations.

Chapter Eight: Sustaining a Mindful Lifestyle

Closing with guidance on maintaining a mindful lifestyle, this chapter emphasizes the ongoing nature of the journey. Discover how small, consistent steps lead to lasting changes, promoting overall health and resilience.

In the fast-paced world we navigate, cultivating a mindful lifestyle is a powerful antidote to the chaos that often engulfs our daily lives. Mindfulness, at its core, is the practice of being fully present, engaged, and aware of each moment without judgment. Integrating mindfulness into our routine can significantly enhance our well-being. Here are practical insights on how to maintain a mindful lifestyle:

Start with the Breath

Begin each day with a few minutes of focused breathing. Pay attention to the inhalation and exhalation, allowing the breath to anchor you to the present moment. This simple practice sets a mindful tone for the day.

Mindful Eating

Transform mealtime into a mindful experience. Engage your senses—observe the colors, textures, and flavors of your food. Chew slowly, savoring each bite. This not only enhances the dining experience but also fosters a deeper connection with your body.

Digital Detox

Designate specific times to unplug from technology. Create sacred spaces free from screens, allowing your mind to unwind and be fully present in the analog world. This break from constant connectivity contributes significantly to mindfulness.

Cultivate Gratitude

Regularly take stock of the positive aspects in your life. Acknowledging and appreciating these moments fosters gratitude. A gratitude journal can be a simple yet powerful tool in recognizing the abundance around you. Name 3 things you are thankful for and WHY you're thankful for them. It isn't enough to simply name things. Getting into the feeling of gratitude is important to making lasting, positive changes.

Mindful Movement

Incorporate mindful movement into your routine, whether it's yoga, tai chi, or a simple walk. Pay attention to the sensations in your body, the rhythm of your movements, and the surrounding environment. Exercise becomes not just a physical activity but a mindful experience.

Single-Tasking

Break free from the habit of multitasking. Focus on one task at a time, fully immersing yourself in it. This not only enhances efficiency but also allows you to appreciate the intricacies of each activity.

Mindful Listening

Practice active listening in your interactions. Truly hear what others are saying without formulating your response while they speak. This fosters deeper connections and enriches your communication.

Nature Connection

Spend time in nature regularly. Whether it's a park, a forest, or a beach, immersing yourself in natural surroundings provides a serene backdrop for mindfulness. Observe the sights, sounds, and sensations of the natural world.

Mindful Reflection

Dedicate a few minutes each day to reflect on your experiences. This self-awareness practice allows you to assess your reactions, emotions, and thought patterns, fostering

personal growth, and understanding.

Evening Mindfulness Routine

Wind down your day with a mindful evening routine. This

could include activities like reading, gentle stretching, or

meditation. Create a peaceful transition from the busyness of the

day to a restful state for a good night's sleep. One way to do this

is just before falling asleep at night, think about your day and

choose the best part of your day.

Embracing a mindful lifestyle is an ongoing journey, and

each small step contributes to a more grounded and fulfilling

existence. By infusing mindfulness into the fabric of your daily life, you cultivate a greater appreciation for the richness of the

present moment.

Chapter Summary/Key Takeaways

- Small, consistent steps towards mindfulness create lasting change.

- Focused breathing brings us into the moment with intentional awareness.

- Mindfulness is a journey that enriches the positive awareness of the present moment.

Epilogue: A Mindful Tomorrow

In the concluding chapter, we reflect on the profound impact of mindfulness on the brain, body, and life as a whole. Readers are inspired to continue their journey towards a mindful and balanced existence, equipped with the knowledge to navigate stress and embrace the beauty of each mindful moment.

About the Author

Debbie has worked in the mental health field for 20 years. Her inspiration is helping people manage life stressors. She understands how stress impacts people's daily lives and how people become caught in negative stress response patterns of behavior. Debbie also understands how to break that negative cycle of behavior.

Debbie earned a Bachelor of Science degree in Criminology; she earned a Master of Arts degree in Psychology & Counseling; she earned a PhD in Counseling Psychology; she earned a Master of Science in Clinical Mental Health Counseling. She has participated in a vast number of trainings and certifications in the mental health field, including Mindfulness-based Stress Reduction.